A World of Languages

by Edward J. Scarry
illustrated by Lyn Martin

PEARSON

Glenview, Illinois • Boston, Massachusetts • Chandler, Arizona
Upper Saddle River, New Jersey

Some people speak only one language. Some people speak many languages.

Knowing another language can help us understand many things. It can help understand what people say, such as greetings like "Hello." Knowing another language can help us understand how people think and feel. It can also help us understand the culture of the people who speak that language.

---

culture: ways of life, including food, celebrations, art, and music

Damian is from Switzerland. He speaks German, French, and Italian. Carol is from the United States. She speaks English and Spanish. Trung is from Vietnam. He speaks Vietnamese and Mandarin.

Some people can speak two or more languages equally well. This usually happens when people learn the languages at a young age.

The first language you learn is your **native** language. This chart shows the five languages that have the most native speakers.

Language	Native Speakers	Main Areas Where Spoken
1 Mandarin	873 million	China, Malaysia, Taiwan
2 English	340 million	United States, United Kingdom, Canada
3 Spanish	322 million	Spain, Latin America
4 Hindi/Urdu	242 million	India
5 Arabic	206 million	Middle East, North Africa

China has the largest population in the world—more than one billion people! That is why Mandarin is the most common language in the world.

---

native: belonging to you because of your nation or ancestors

Damian lives in Switzerland. He speaks German, French, and Italian. These are the three main languages spoken in his country.

Damian has visited many places in his country. He has also visited Switzerland's neighbors: Germany, Austria, Italy, and France. Damian is happy he can understand the language and culture of so many different places.

Carol lives in the United States. Her native language is English. She also speaks Spanish. Spanish is the language of Mexico. Mexico is south of the United States. Carol likes Mexican culture—especially the food and music!

Sometimes Carol helps **translate** words for her friends who do not speak Spanish.

---

translate: to change from one language into another

Trung lives in Vietnam. His native language is Vietnamese. He also speaks Mandarin. Mandarin is a Chinese language. China is north of Vietnam.

Trung likes to go to Chinese restaurants and speak Mandarin with the people there. And he likes to eat the tasty food, too!

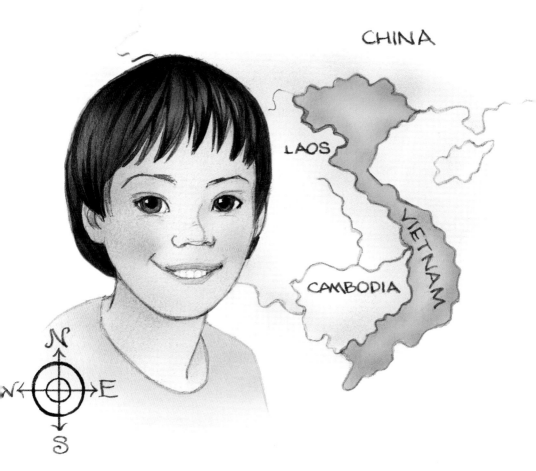

The world has many different languages and cultures. Sometimes this can cause problems. Sometimes people do not understand each other. Sometimes a different culture seems strange.

But Damian, Carol, and Trung show us that language and culture do not have to separate people. Language and culture can link people from all over the world. They can also help people learn from one another.

---

separate: to divide or keep apart